A SPIRIT DAUGHTER
WORKBOOK

WRITTEN BY
JILL WINTERSTEEN

FOR THE FULL MOON

SUNDAY, AUGUST 22ND, 2021
5:01AM PT

THE AGE OF AQUARIUS

The cosmos always gives us what we need. There are no accidents and there are no coincidences. It's all meant to be. This year, we have two Full Moons in Aquarius, giving us an opportunity to understand this energy more fully, shed the lower frequencies of the sign, and align with the highest vibrations it has to offer. Aquarius, in many ways, is the energy we need right now as a society to help us evolve, restructure, and shift paradigms. It is the vibration that will guide us as we ascend to a new level of existence and shift out of lower vibrations like racism, sexism, bigotry, chauvinism, homophobia, and xenophobia. Aquarius has the power to help us feel connected to all beings and make choices that empower everyone. In its highest manifestation, Aquarius helps us all live our truths while honoring other people's truths, even if our truths don't agree with theirs. It's about seeing differences while also living in an energy of equality.

It also seems cosmically guided that we have two Full Moons in Aquarius as we begin to embrace the Age of Aquarius. Astrological ages last for about 2,000 years, and they move backward through the astrological wheel. We have been in the Pisces Age for roughly the last 2,000 years. The ages are determined by the placement of the Sun on the vernal equinox. Without getting too technical, the exact beginning of the Age of Aquarius is a hotly debated topic. Some astrologers argue that is began in the first half of the twentieth century when we saw the first flight and other technological advances like radio broadcasting and television, which connected us

THE AGE OF AQUARIUS

all. Others have argued it began in 2011 with the shifting of the star Regulus, while others claim it won't begin until 2600. Then there is the current opinion that the Age of Aquarius is beginning right now, ushered in by a global pandemic and the great December 2020 conjunction of Saturn and Jupiter in Aquarius. Furthermore, Saturn and Jupiter will meet in Air signs for the next 200 years, bringing us a planetary Air age. The current Air age is not the same thing as the Age of Aquarius, but it is helping us align with this new astrological age and understand how it is changing us.

Whether we are already in the Age of Aquarius or it's about to begin, this energy is taking over the collective and shifting the vibration of everyone on the planet. Great transformations are not easy, and this shift will not be a comfortable one. It's important to believe with all of your energy that any and all of the struggles we are seeing society go through is for the greater evolution of all people. Paradigm shifts of any kind require trust and faith. It's up to each of us on an individual level to keep our vibrations high and emit them to the world, especially in times of crisis. This, of course, takes dedication on our parts to do the work to align with a higher frequency.

As we move into the Age of Aquarius, it's important to understand your energetic field. Your energy affects every being around you. It affects people, pets, plants, water, and anything that carries an energetic charge. Yes, you affect your crystals just as much as they affect you. As we begin to understand the power of our energy and the innate power we hold, we can begin to understand our responsibility to take care of our energy. Aquarius is ruled by Air, and air connects us all. It helps us share ideas, emotions, and energy. Begin to think about how you connect with the world around you in terms of energy. This includes understanding that you give and receive energy from various sources.

Some examples of living energetically are looking at the ocean and breathing in some of her power when you feel drained. Or when having a conversation with someone, elevating their thinking by sending them energy as they speak. If you want to see a change happen in your life, cultivate the energy that it already happened. If you want to see a change happen in the world, be that change and all the energy it carries. Yes, you may still have to take action when needed, but take action from a place rooted in the energy you want to manifest. If you want to see more love in the world, speak about love from a place of love. Great movements are created by people who know who they are, understand their energy, and have a vision of the future. That vision includes aligning with energy that creates the change needed to bring their dreams into reality.

The Age of Aquarius asks us to take a leap and view the world a bit differently. It asks that we view it from the lens of energy. It also asks that you find out who you are and understand your own frequency. Aquarius wants us to be ourselves in every situation. This individuality inspires other people to find their own sense of self. It's also what changes the world. And love ties it all together. When everyone is aligned with their authentic selves from a place of love, they are accepting of both themselves and others. In the true vision of Aquarius, each person in the collective is unique and different while contributing their individuality to shaping society. We each have a part to play in the grand puzzle of life. Aquarius helps us recognize our piece and embody it while accepting everyone else for who they are. The Age of Aquarius represents the oneness we can obtain if we are willing to connect our minds with our hearts and create societal frameworks from this perspective. This vision includes the notion that everyone is valued for what they offer, which is different from person to person. There is no better or worse when we think about people—there is only love and oneness. Welcome to the Age of Aquarius.

04

TRADITIONAL RULERS & MODERN RULERS
OF THE SIGNS

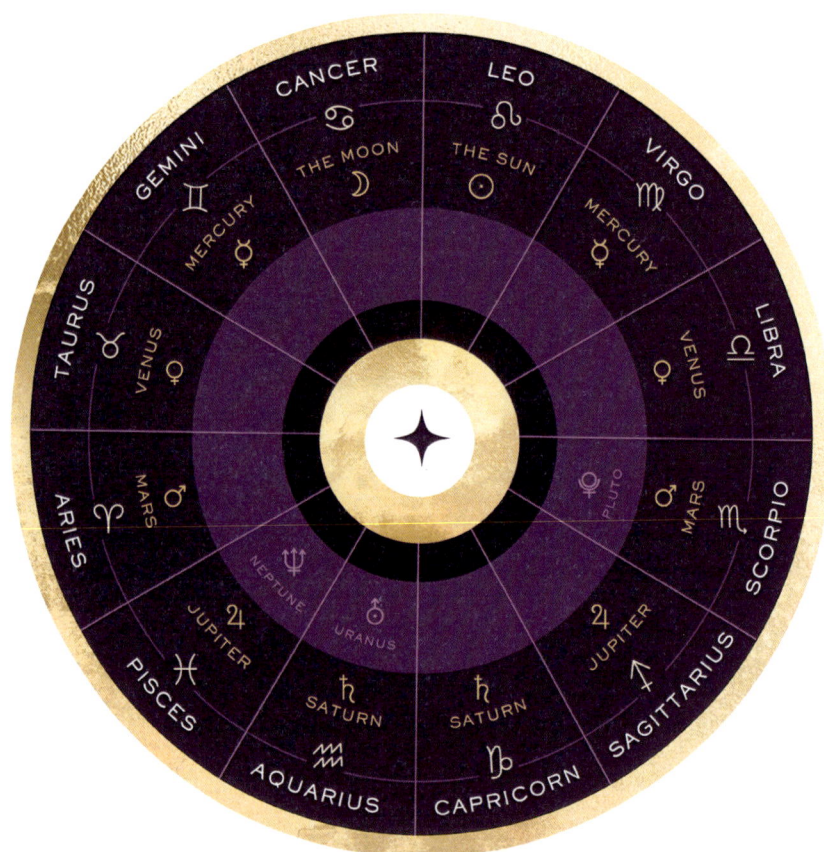

TRADITIONAL RULERS

THE MOON RULES CANCER
THE SUN RULES LEO
MERCURY RULES GEMINI & VIRGO
VENUS RULES TAURUS & LIBRA
MARS RULES ARIES & SCORPIO
JUPITER RULES PISCES & SAGITTARIUS
SATURN RULES AQUARIUS & CAPRICORN

MODERN RULERS

NEPTUNE IS THE MODERN RULER OF PISCES
URANUS IS THE MODERN RULER OF AQUARIUS
PLUTO IS THE MODERN RULER OF SCORPIO

AQUARIUS FULL MOON

Aquarius is a multifaceted energy, and on this second Full Moon in its sign, we get to dive a bit deeper into understanding it. Aquarius is best understood through exploring the planets that rule it. Aquarius, like Scorpio and Pisces, has a modern ruling planet and a traditional one. Astrology is thousands of years old, and up until the advent of telescopes, the only planets anyone knew about were the ones that could be seen with the naked eye. In 1781, Uranus was the first planet beyond Saturn to be discovered, and it wasn't until the late 1800s or early 1900s that astrologers placed it as the ruling planet of Aquarius. Until this point, Saturn was the ruler of Aquarius. Even today some traditional astrologers still consider Saturn the ruling planet, and some modern astrologers won't even consider Saturn's influence on the water bearer.

SATURN

Astrologers continue to debate which planet rules Aquarius, but when we look deeply into Aquarius's energy, we can see both Saturn's and Uranus's influences. Considering both planets as its ruler also helps us understand the rather dual nature of this Air sign. Saturn governs the rules of society and its structure. Saturn is conservative in its energy. It wants to maintain the status quo and conserve the values of a given society. Saturn's energy can feel cold and aloof. It constantly reminds us that there are consequences to every action and that those consequences affect everyone around us. Saturn, though, ultimately doesn't care what we do because we are the ones who have to live with our choices. Saturn also rules karma and teaches us that what goes around comes around.

Saturn, though, does encourage us to make choices with others in mind. It helps us understand the interconnected web we all live in. Even decisions that seem to affect only us or our immediate family ripple out into the world and change people's lives who we may not even know. Anytime laws are instilled, Saturn's energy is there to guide the process. Saturn helps us understand the need for regulations and governing bodies that ensure the safety of all people. Saturn helps us create ways to ensure that karma is not the only repercussion for poor choices. It helps us grow as a society and evolve as humans through creating systems that allow us to function together as a unified whole.

Planets flavor, or give themes to, the signs they rule. The signs then go on and motivate the behaviors of people with this energy. Saturn influences the side of Aquarius that governs group dynamics and the collective consciousness. Saturn adds structure and order to Aquarius's signature, and Aquarius then encourages people to become leaders and create societal infrastructures. But all of that gets a little boring, which is where we meet Uranus, the planet that shake things up and encourages people to rebel against the very systems its co-ruler put in place. Aquarius, though, still needs Saturn, even with its new and improved ruler Uranus, because without Saturn there would be nothing to challenge, change, and evolve.

change is part
of the adventure.

AQUARIUS FULL MOON

�uranus symbol

URANUS

Upon its discovery, Uranus shook the foundation of both astronomy and astrology. It broke the rules of the sky and caused people of that time to think differently. It evolved science and our collective consciousness. It also caused quite a dispute among astrologers. Where could this new planet fit in? Until the discovery of Uranus, Saturn ruled both Capricorn and Aquarius energies. But astrology is built on observation, and it's very clear that people born under Capricorn influences and people born under Aquarius influences were very different. Furthermore, when the Sun landed in Aquarius, there was a clear shift in energy. Capricorn's Sun Season brought order, solitude, and perseverance through the winter, while Aquarius's Sun Season brought people out of their homes to gather with friends and share in ideas on how to navigate the world. In these meetings, systems were born and rules were broken. Clearly, Aquarius contained a different energy compared to Capricorn, and that energy was Uranus. Uranus was then declared the modern ruler of Aquarius and changed astrology as we know it.

Uranus influences the side of Aquarius that cracks the very foundation we all stand on. When we align with this side of Aquarius, we question everything. Uranus helps us see every side of the puzzle of life and opens our minds to new perspectives. If you ever need help solving a problem, call on Uranus's energy to help you think outside the box and realize there actually is no box. Uranus imbues Aquarius with the energy that gives rise to visionaries and people who can see far into the future. This aspect of Aquarius helps progress society forward into a new paradigm. It helps us envision a completely different world with new structures and systems. If we are ever to get out of the current climate crisis, it will be Uranus and Aquarius that help us form a new paradigm around energy usage in which we redefine resources and how to use them. Uranus is the energy of major societal change, and its influence on Aquarius motivates protests, eye-opening conversations, and the exchange of ideas that elevate the collective to a new point of existence.

On a Full Moon, we are working not only with the signs involved, but also their rulers. On this second Full Moon in Aquarius, feel into the energies of both Saturn and Uranus. Feel into what you need to break away from in your life. How can you break through outdated thinking to invent new ways to solve issues? Additionally, how can understanding advanced concepts like energy and frequency help you evolve your thinking? Uranus helps us understand the future, and the future is energy. What can you do today to think in more energetic terms? How are you shaping yourself and your world with the frequency you emit? As you find the higher vibrations of Aquarius, feel how the simple act of thinking in terms of energy is changing the paradigms we all live in. If you're feeling blocked try an energetic solution. Instead of using logic to find an answer, call it in with your energy. Cultivate a frequency within you that reflects what you want to attract. Do the work internally, emit it outward, and attract what you need. A bonus is that you'll also contribute your positive vibration to the collective pool of energy, helping raise the vibration of the world.

AQUARIUS MOON X LEO SUN

Throughout this Full Moon, we have the opportunity to raise our frequency by working with both the energy of Leo, where the Sun is positioned, and the energy of Aquarius, where the Moon lands. This Full Moon allows us to fully integrate the higher vibrations of both of these signs while releasing their lower frequencies from our energetic fields. As we shift our energy with the help of the Full Moon, we can bring awareness to our outdated patterns and make space to form new ones that more accurately represent who we are and the energy we want to emit to the world.

The highest vibration of Leo and Aquarius is unconditional love for all beings, including love for ourselves and others. True acceptance leads to true belonging for all people. The key to achieving this high vibrational state is releasing the lower vibrations. This part requires some shadow work. Shadow work helps us make the unconscious conscious. It allows us to peer into the subconscious and find our emotional triggers, the origins of our reactions, and our judgments. Shadow work is the work of every Full Moon. Under the Moon's light we can see the energies we embody that block our highest potential and visions. The Full Moon helps us shed light on our shadows to transform and release them.

Every energy has a low side and a high side. Through understanding the lower vibrations of both Leo and Aquarius, we can feel into how we align with them in our lives. The Full Moon helps us see where these energies show up. This awareness is the first and most important step in shifting our shadows into the light of higher frequencies.

While the highest manifestation of Leo and Aquarius is unconditional love, their lower frequencies range from extreme aloofness to dramatic attention-seeking behavior. Leo and Aquarius create a range of frequencies. On one end is the extreme side of Aquarius, and on the other is the extreme side of Leo. Our job this Full Moon is to let go of these extreme, or low, sides and find a balance point in the middle that embodies these signs' higher frequencies. This work can be uncomfortable, but it is pivotal for your energetic evolution. As you recognize where the lower frequencies are showing up for you, you can release them from your field. Have compassion for yourself through this process and be grateful for your willingness to transform.

Leo's lower vibration, or shadow side, leaves the high vibration of love and enters the shadow of the ego. The ego can be a good thing: it provides self-esteem and helps us define our . It is the basis of our identity. "I" statements and helps us stay focused on what's most important to our growth. A healthy ego can increase our willpower and give us confidence during challenging circumstances. It also helps us be vulnerable and admit how we feel from the "I" perspective. Statements like "I don't know" or, "I'm sorry" come from the ego.

While the ego can be a strength, it can also be a weakness. When the ego takes a turn for the dark side, we end up aligning with the low sides of Leo: arrogance, neediness, and closed-hearted living. When our egos get out of control, we lack vulnerability and cannot admit fault. We live in fear of rejection from others to the point where we can't take accountability for our actions. We also overexert our will on others, attempting to control them and force their approval. This may look like dramatic behavior to gain attention or manipulate praise. We become needy and unaware of the pressure we put on others to validate our talents. In this frequency, our self-acceptance becomes interlinked with the outside world. We forget that the only approval we need is our own and become a performer feigning authenticity for the applause of others.

LET LOVE LEAD EVERY DECISION

AQUARIUS MOON X LEO SUN

If you find yourself in the lower vibrations of Leo, marked by an unbalanced ego, bring yourself back to center by defining who you are. Write a list of "I" statements that define you. Admit your strengths and weaknesses. You can include statements like "I am sorry for ..." or "I am wise" or "I am loving" or "I am causing drama because ..." or "I am scared." You can decide on the list, but the purpose is to put your ego in check by speaking directing from it and your heart. As you make this list, accept who you are and love yourself. Share some of this information with others and allow them to accept and love you too—organically and without any drama or manipulation.

Aquarius, like Leo, also has a lower side to its energy: aloofness and disconnection. Aquarius teaches us that we each have the power to change the world by showing up in our truth. When we align with the low side of Aquarius, we forget our power and retreat from the world. We become aloof and withdraw our energy from the collective. We leave it up to others to change systems and structures that govern all of us. We withhold our ideas not because we don't think people will like them, but because we don't feel like contributing them. We lose our inspiration to incite change and instead live our lives the way we want. Yes, there is personal freedom in this low side, but it's to an extreme. It's the type of freedom that breaks away us from society and leaves the world to fend for itself.

When we align with the most extreme side of Aquarius, we sit on the sidelines and judge others who are trying to change the status quo. This side grants us many opinions, and we may even share them, but in a nonconstructive way. When we align with this frequency, we forget to take personal responsibility for the problems around us. We blame the larger organizations that govern and spin tales of what "should" be done instead of realizing we contribute to the greater whole. One clue that you are aligning with this vibration is when you start blaming others for things you could change yourself. Blaming is a disempowering energy, in which we forget that we are just as powerful as and equal to the people making the rules that dictate our personal freedom. We each have a responsibility to contribute our uniqueness, voice, and greatness to the world. If we all do this, we change the frequency of the planet.

If you find yourself aligning with the lower frequencies of Aquarius, get involved in something. Find something that you believe in and can support with your energy. Empower yourself to contribute your intelligence and energy to shaping the world we all live in. And choose something that resonates with your soul and allows you to express your individuality. This may be through volunteering or creating a platform to educate others about something. It may look like getting involved in your local community or even learning more about how you can get involved. You may become a leader of a movement or a much needed supporter of a cause. Either way, contributing your energy to evolving the collective will help you shift away from the lower frequency of Aquarius.

As you become aware of the lower frequencies of both Leo and Aquarius, you can shift them in your energetic field to higher vibrations. On this second Full Moon in Aquarius, feel your capacity to evolve society to a new level of existence by doing the work on yourself to raise your vibration. Feel your capacity for unconditional love of all people and let this love lead every decision.

ASPECTS

The main aspect of every Full Moon is the opposition of the Sun and Moon. There are other planets in the sky, though, and they affect the Full Moon, especially when they aspect it. Planetary aspects occur when specific angles are formed between cosmic bodies. For instance, trine aspects form when cosmic bodies are 120° away from each other. Squares form when they are 90° away from each other, and oppositions occur when they are 180° away from each other in the sky.

Along with the opposition of the Sun and Moon, Jupiter also opposes the Sun this Full Moon and forms a conjunction with the Moon. Conjunctions occur when cosmic bodies are within 7° of each other. Jupiter expands everything it touches. It shows us our potential and asks where we are not living up to it. Jupiter wants us to be great and to take up space. Jupiter teaches us how to break through self-imposed limitations and take leaps to higher levels of existence.

Jupiter is retrograde this Full Moon, meaning its energy takes a more inward focus. Jupiter retrograde teaches us that happiness is an inside job. Our expansion comes from our own ability to imagine it. We need to believe with every fiber of our being that we are capable of great things. This transit helps us release doubt and recognize places where we are keeping ourselves small, and why. There are many reasons we avoid our potential. Fear is one of them. We often fear success much more than failure because we don't know who we will be if we succeed. We also fear the unknown. Even if we think we want our visions to manifest, we sometimes sabotage them because we are not ready for change. Many of our blocks are subconscious, but Jupiter retrograde can bring them to the surface.

With Jupiter Retrograde aspecting this Full Moon, we are asked to look at how we limit ourselves. What things do you tell yourself about growth and your potential? Jupiter Retrograde is in Aquarius, with the Moon bringing up issues like how you allow the collective to dictate your behaviors. Are you letting society tell you who you can be and what your potential is? Harness the energy of this aspect to break free of preconceived notions of who you should be. Feel into how you may be changing yourself or keeping yourself small to fit in or please other people. Look into subconscious patterns to guide you to conform with the status quo while stifling your expansion. Growth can be uncomfortable, but fitting in places you've outgrown is far worse. Allow yourself to evolve this Full Moon, even if it means you no longer fit in with the collective. Your willingness to grow will encourage everyone around you to do the same.

We currently have five planets in retrograde: Jupiter, Saturn, Uranus, Neptune, and Pluto. Cosmically, we are on repeat as planets dance around each other, reminding us that there is no linear road available. Life moves in cycles, the Universe moves in cycles. Retrogrades bring us lessons to reintegrate and help us process events more deeply. See repeating cycles as an opportunity to learn, unlearn, and heal. Also, recognize that movement happens in all directions. The key is to keep moving.

Saturn Retrograde helps us notice circumstances that seem to be on repeat. Become aware of what your karma is calling into your world so you can find resolution with an old attachment. Also, clear your karma with others. Take responsibility for your actions and your role in situations that didn't turn out as you'd hoped. Learn what you need to from others with an open mind and willingness to listen to their side. Also, learn what you need from yourself. How can you look at a situation differently to understand it from another angle? As you resolve your karma, you pull your energy into the present moment. You detach from the past and make your entire vibration available to you in the here and now. As you free yourself of energetic attachments, you take control of your frequency and in turn vibrate higher. When we are not spending time thinking about the past, we are free to fully step into the present. The full spectrum of our energy becomes available to us to direct, harness, and create the life we want. We can commit with confidence and contribute to the rise of the collective vibration. Saturn Retrograde asks, What commitments do you need to release to embrace ones that support your current self?

Uranus's energy can feel jarring to the nervous system, as it brings us into the unknown. With Uranus there is no easing into it; this planet's energy is bold and confrontational. It throws us right into the deep end, then expects us to develop a new method of swimming to navigate the waters. Uranus Retrograde asks us to rethink how and why we are doing things. It asks us to reevaluate our dreams from a different perspective. Life is constantly changing. Our visions need to change with it. What was true yesterday may not be true today. Over this Full Moon, ask yourself if you are viewing yourself or the collective from an outdated lens. Uranus Retrograde asks, How can you update your visions to match the current reality?

Neptune is the planet of dreams. While retrograde, it asks us to feel into our dreams and visions and decide which ones resonate with our souls. There is a subtle difference between dreams and fantasy. We may spend some time fantasizing about lives we could live, but at the end of the day these fantasies are just escapes. They do not resonate with our true essence and the reason we are alive. Neptune Retrograde helps us reassess our dreams and decide which ones are worth putting our attention on and which ones are simply a pleasant distraction. Neptune Retrograde asks, Where has your imagination betrayed you and how can you focus on what's most important?

Pluto Retrograde allows us to reprocess events in our lives that were once labeled painful or even traumatic. In its highest light, Pluto teaches us to honor the ongoing cycles of the Universe. We see the ebb and flow of life itself and learn to trust it. Pluto helps us understand the deeper meaning of things and shows us how to interpret energies differently. For instance, Pluto introduces us to the idea that sometimes seemingly negative events occur to actually block even harsher realities from unfolding. Pluto reorganizes the way we view pain and even death, reminding us that we are eternal beings and this lifetime is part of a series of lifetimes. Our energy is on a constant quest of evolution, and it is never lost, only found again. During this Full Moon, let go of outdated perspectives of your past that are constraining you. See where your expansion and evolution are blocked by attachments to past events or the inability to process them. Become aware of where your past is constraining you and free yourself. Pluto Retrograde asks, How do you step away from your past and fly to your potential?

14

SATURN PLACEMENTS

You are probably well aware of your Sun sign and even Moon sign. These are the zodiac constellations the Sun and Moon were positioned in when you were born. You also have a Saturn sign, along with a Mercury, Venus, and so on. Your Saturn sign, or placement, is the zodiac constellation Saturn was positioned in when you were born. You can find your Saturn sign at astro-charts.com in your natal chart.

Your natal chart is a picture of the sky when you were born. It is composed of twelve pieces, or houses; planets in those houses; and signs governing them. The planets represent aspects of your personality, while the signs motivate those pieces in a certain direction. Your houses are areas of your life these pieces of your personality show up and act in.

In your chart, Saturn governs the part of you that feels a responsibility to your karmic path and to other people. Understanding your Saturn placement gives information about what you feel called to do this in this life and what you feel most responsible for. It can also help you understand what is your perceived duty and how that affects the rest of your actions.

As we journey through this Full Moon in Aquarius, it may bring up feelings around your responsibilities and how you want to shift them. Saturn is the traditional ruler of Aquarius. When the Full Moon activates Aquarius, it also activates your Saturn, calling your attention to it. You may be able to understand your Saturn placement more deeply today, and in turn understand how to embrace your karmic responsibility this lifetime. Below is guidance on what your Saturn placements can teach you about yourself, your life, and your personality.

Saturn in Aries: Your responsibility this lifetime is to yourself and your mission. You face challenges head on and understand that your path will be full of highs and lows. You stay committed to your journey no matter what curveballs come your way. It's important to never let fear or worst-case scenarios make your decisions. Anything done from fear will feel like a betrayal to your authentic self. You are strong and resilient, and you keep your eye on the prize. You are willing to sacrifice many things to obtain your goals; just remember to never sacrifice your commitments to yourself.

Saturn in Taurus: Your responsibility this lifetime is to cultivate peace and serenity for yourself. In order to follow through on any commitment, you need a strong foundation and a feeling of safety. Once you have these things in place, you are capable of great focus and creativity. Your path includes honoring your talent for building. You can build almost anything, from the perfect garden to the well-orchestrated piece of music. And you feel a karmic duty to build great works for both yourself and the world around you. Just remember that it all starts with stillness within you.

Saturn in Gemini: Your responsibility this lifetime is to communicate yourself effectively and clearly. You have many ideas and are here to learn how to voice them. Your most rewarding commitments center around learning and evolving your perceptions through asking the right questions. Your voice is your power, and you can center many of your life's ambitions around it. Focus your energy on learning how to refine your voice and use it to create the change you wish to see in the world. Just remember that when you silence yourself, you betray yourself. Always speak your truth even when it ruffles some feathers.

(continued on next page)

SATURN PLACEMENTS

Saturn in Cancer: Your responsibility this lifetime is to take care of yourself. You are here in this lifetime to heal and love yourself. Commit to being kind to yourself; rest when you need it, cry when you need it, and always give yourself space to feel. Fill your life with people and activities that replenish your soul. Make this nurturing your priority and know that when you do, you become an example of self-care for others to follow. You also have a great capacity for helping others and can become quite focused on your healing work. Healing is your gift, and you give it to others freely. Just remember to never place your own healing second to anyone's else's.

Saturn in Leo: Your responsibility is to your creativity. You are here to express yourself to others and show them your inner world. This type of vulnerability requires courage and commitment. When you hide your true self, it feels like a betrayal to your soul. It is your duty to spread joy and love to others through your expressions. You have a great capacity for lifting the vibration of any room if you are willing to bare your soul and share your true self. Stay focused on being yourself and recognizing your unique talent. Commit to unconditional love of yourself. Just remember that you do not need the approval of other people to be yourself.

Saturn in Virgo: Your responsibility this lifetime is to share your gifts with others. Furthermore, you need to share them in a way that others can understand and integrate easily. You have a great capacity for healing the collective. You were born with a natural talent to heal. Much of this healing occurs from the information you are able to digest, organize, and give back to others. You can present complicated topics with great ease. This is just one of your many gifts and ways you heal. Focus on your strengths and release any self-criticism. Know that you hold vast wisdom and that others are waiting for it. Just remember how worthy your ideas and energy are to the collective.

Saturn in Libra: Your responsibility this lifetime is to create balance in your life. This balance comes from your external environment, your inner landscape, and your relationships. You are committed to peace in your life. Focus your energy on creating beautiful spaces that feel supportive to your energy. Likewise, cultivate relationships that feel supportive by embracing partners who understand your need for balance. Then extend this peace to the collective. You may find yourself working in law or some form of activism. You have a strong commitment to create peace in the world and often find creative ways to do it. Just remember that peace begins within.

SATURN PLACEMENTS

Saturn in Scorpio: Your responsibility this lifetime is to the truth. You are on a mission to understand the true nature of yourself, others, and the world. You do not shy away from the depths of existence, but rather plunge headfirst into them. You understand innately when someone is lying, even if that person is yourself. You feel a commitment to reveal any untruths. And you often find yourself exposing people for who they really are. No one can fool you. You can see past any façade, and your duty this lifetime is to break down anything that isn't real. Just remember to do it with some kindness.

Saturn in Sagittarius: Your responsibility this lifetime is to expand. You are here to break free of any comfort zones and travel into the unknown. You feel a natural pull from your soul to explore the world and experience as many new things as possible. If you betray this instinct, you will end up feeling stuck, stagnant, and frustrated. As you expand your horizons, there is a subsequent responsibility to share what you learn with the world. You are a wonderful teacher, philosopher, and storyteller. You may find yourself with a large community that wants to learn from you, as you will experience more than most. Just remember to keep exploring even when things get interesting at home.

Saturn in Capricorn: Your responsibility this lifetime is to your life's work. You are here on a mission, and you've known this your whole life. You have the ability to focus through the most difficult circumstances and are never intimidated by a challenge. You know you can accomplish great things, and you do. Your commitments are strong, and anything you place your mind on gets your full attention. You also need to remember to take care of yourself, though. In striving for excellence, you may create an unbalanced life. Begin to understand that self-care feeds your work and enhances it. Your life is full of great feats; just remember to make restoring your spirit one of your many accomplishments.

Saturn in Aquarius: Your responsibility this lifetime is to contribute something unique to the collective. You see the world through a different lens than most people. With these insights you have the power to move the world forward. Your questions and challenges of societal norms serve you well in creating visions of the future. Once you have a vision, you commit all of your energy to it. Your duty this lifetime is to help others see a new world. You are a leader and you work hard to spread your inspiration to the collective. Not everyone will understand your hard work to change the future, but you will, and that's all that counts. Just remember to not be offended when others give you questioning glances. You're also going through your Saturn return right now while Saturn lands in Aquarius. This is a time of great growth for you. It's also a time when you will feel the long-term consequences of every action you take. You may change careers, partners, or even cities now. It's all to better align you with your soul's commitments. What do you want to be responsible to and for now, five years from now, and even in the next decade?

Saturn in Pisces: Your responsibility this lifetime is to your spiritual growth. You have the keen ability to focus on spiritual paths, such as meditation, yoga, or other disciplines. You can train your mind in these areas to a higher degree than most people. With this intense focus, you evolve much more on a spiritual level than most people. This wisdom makes you a powerful healer. You may even find your life's work revolving around healing. You can sit with others for lengths of time and give them the energy they need to heal. Once you hone this skill, you can heal others without feeling drained or taking on their pain. This type of energetic healing takes dedication, but you have the constitution for it. Just remember that not everyone will be ready for the healing you offer; it is too powerful for some.

18

URANUS PLACEMENTS

In addition to Saturn and the other planets, we also have a Uranus sign, or placement, in our natal chart. It takes Uranus eighty-four years to orbit the Sun, which means it remains in an astrological sign for seven to eight years, depending on its retrogrades. Uranus was discovered in 1781, when it broke down the dominating thoughts about the solar system. Also ringed like Saturn, Uranus is tilted so far on its side that it appears to be rolling instead of spinning on its axis. Uranus defied conventional thought about the sky. It caused astrologers and astronomers to break down what they thought was possible and incorporate new knowledge. Uranus brought the unexpected to science, and it brings the unexpected to your life.

Uranus in your chart shows where you need to break through something in this lifetime. It tells you where you need to use your imagination and unique genius to change an energy you brought with you from a past life. Uranus governs your unconventional thoughts and the vibrations you embrace that differ from the norm. Look to your Uranus if you feel stuck or stagnant somewhere. This lack of flow can be an indication that something needs to shift. Uranus will be right there to help you enter a new reality.

Uranus in your chart also shows what may show up unexpectedly in your life. These events may be uncomfortable, painful, or simply surprising. They will, however, change you dramatically—usually for the better. Even if they seem challenging at first, situations brought by Uranus are meant to break you out of an outdated pattern and show you a new light. Uranus is shocking, and that shock can feel like you stuck your finger in an electric socket, but all in all it's a good thing. Uranus has the ability to change you dramatically, and that change may be just what you need to evolve to the next level.

The following are descriptions of Uranus placements. You can look yours up at astro-charts.com. With the Full Moon in Aquarius, the area of the chart governed by Uranus is activated. You may feel earthquakes in this area, or you may be in for an unexpected surprise. Either way, take it with grace and know that change is on the horizon. Growth is always uncomfortable, but it's necessary for your evolution.

Uranus in Aries (1927–1935; 2010–2019)
You are here to shatter preconceived notions about the self. You break the rules of identity and surprise others through the way you represent yourself. You stand up for yourself with great conviction and use your will wisely to make a point. You defend your choices vigorously and can have quite a temper when it comes to making your point known. You courageously show new and unexpected ways of identifying yourself within the collective. Be bold and know that you are breaking through outdated patterns to free others to be themselves.

Uranus in Taurus (1935–1942; 2019–2026)
You are here to break through ideas about Mother Earth and her resources. You have the making of someone born to be an environmental activist. You understand the language of nature more deeply than most people. You make friends with the animal kingdom and make it a priority to defend it. You also understand money and currency from a different framework. Topics like cryptocurrency are natural to you, and you make money through unconventional methods. You see the future when it comes to all resources and have a vision of what a new, evolved Earth could look like once we learn to take better care of her.

(continued on next page)

You can look up where Uranus is in your chart, at astro-charts.com

URANUS PLACEMENTS

Uranus in Gemini (1942–1949; 2025–2033)
You are here to inspire new forms of communication. You understand all forms of language, even unconventional ones, like body language or energetic transmissions. You may even surprise people in your life with your psychic nature. You also think differently than most people, seeing things from different angles. You surprise people with your insights and perceptions. Not all will be ready for it, and it's up to you to know that's ok. You also are given many events in your life that challenge you to use your voice. Some may be unexpected but all will ask you to defy your common methods of communication and find a new way to express your insights.

Uranus in Cancer (1948–1956; 2032–2040)
You are here to break people's assumptions about feelings. You have the capacity to feel all emotions, and in unique ways. You understand emotions at a deeper and different level than most. With this knowledge, you can guide others in understanding their emotions from a different angle and with a different lens. You also help redefine the meaning of family. You may not have a traditional family, but you have plenty of love in your life just the same. You help society redefine what family means and how it interacts with that paradigm.

Uranus in Leo (1955–1962; 2039–2045)
You are here to break through vulnerability. You use your witty and humorous expression to say the things others are thinking but don't dare speak. You are honest, open, and unfiltered. You have compassion with your words, but you don't hold back. You have no shame or fear of embarrassment, for you know you are redefining self-expression. You say unexpected things in unexpected ways—often to the surprise of everyone around you. Although you may be a bit dramatic, you are always truthful. Others may not be ready to support or receive your vulnerability, and that's ok. They may catch up at some point. Just keep being an example of what it means to wear your heart on your sleeve.

Uranus in Virgo (1961–1969)
You are here to defy methods of healing. You break out of the conventional models and embrace alternative medicines. Your end goal is to be of service to others, and you seek to accomplish this in novel ways. You experiment with forms of energetic healing, such as acupuncture, reiki, and other forms of energetic medicine. You will try anything in the name of healing, then you bring your findings to the collective. You have the capacity to shift paradigms around medicine and medical technologies if you are willing to challenge the status quo. You may also encounter health challenges in your life that lead to the discovery of new forms of medicine. Trust your intuition to guide you, even when science has not proven your theories yet. They'll catch up.

Uranus in Libra (1968–1975)
You are here to break the rules and assumptions around partnerships. You embrace unexpected partners and often meet them through unconventional methods. You have a great appreciation for everyone on this planet and see everyone as equal. You are a champion for inclusivity and the rights of all partnerships, no matter if others label them as untraditional. You also break the mold on beauty and help usher in new trends in the area of art and fashion. You create unexpected modalities to showcase beauty in all forms. You are capable of expanding the collective's idea of what and who is beautiful. All around, you present a diverse and inclusive world to others who may be limited in their definitions of beauty and love.

Uranus in Scorpio (1974–1981)
You are here to break the rules around the unseen. You understand the depth of the human psyche from a unique perspective. You are not afraid to talk about taboo subjects such as sex, death, and money. What you are afraid of is not living in your

truth. You seek to understand the basis of your consciousness, as well as the collective's. You go to great lengths to make the unconscious conscious. No topic is off limits for you; you want to explore it all and make it seen to everyone. You often encourage the world to strengthen its research areas in certain topics and to start talking about things that were once hidden. You bring everything to light. You also attract challenging circumstances that cause you to evolve at a rapid pace and find out how strong you really are in the face of the unthinkable.

Uranus in Sagittarius (1981–1988)
You are here to break through conventional definitions of the meaning of life. From a young age, you've questioned the governing authorities' view of the world and have made a quest to find your own purpose. You challenge the status quo around what makes people feel happy and fulfilled. You do not believe anything you were taught about how to define happiness. You break away from conventional paths of life and seek to pave your own path to a life filled with joy and contentment. Your parents may have some questions about the choices you've made, but ultimately it's your life. Just maybe you'll teach them something about what it means to find happiness and meaning.

Uranus in Capricorn (1988–1996)
You are here to break traditional concepts of work and career. You most likely reject or at least don't agree with the forty-hour work week. You also don't understand the concept of an office. Remote work makes complete sense to you, and you don't understand why everyone hasn't worked like this for years. You also don't subscribe to traditional career ladders, and you believe you can reinvent your career at any time. You may even hold an unconventional job or start a company that breaks the mold of business. You want to love what you do each day, and you have a complete understanding that if you don't like your job, you don't like your life. You want your career and your life's work to be the same, and you are redefining the meaning of "job" as you merge the two.

Uranus in Aquarius (1995–2003)
You are here to break through outdated societal programs. You see the world from a unique perspective, including issues involving the collective. You are a visionary and can see the future for all people. You seek to spend your life creating change for society and shifting old programming that no longer makes sense to you. You are also fluent in technology. Having never known a world without the internet, you understand technology to a greater degree than people older than you. In your highest expression, you have the potential to merge your knowledge of technology with ideas on how the world needs to change. How can we use our technological advances to progress society forward, including changing the way we use our Earth's resources? Likewise, how can our technology help ensure that all people are supported, treated equally, and honored for their differences in the collective? These are questions you can answer and may have to answer in your lifetime.

Uranus in Pisces (2003–2011)
You are here to break through the current limiting beliefs around spirituality. You belong to the "new" New Age, as you bring the collective novel approaches to spiritual practices. You have the ability to connect with the Universal Consciousness on a deeper level than most. This wisdom comes to you in the form of unexpected psychic hits and strange encounters. From an early age, you have been able to connect dots about human consciousness that scholars have been wrestling with for years. While those around you may not understand your knowledge, it is highly valuable to the evolution of society. You can teach others how to connect with the Universe and how to understand the interconnectedness of all beings. You can usher us into the world of energy and bring a new understanding of how to connect with each other, our intuition, and civilizations that came before us. You just may shift us into another dimension of existence.

CIRCLE SET UP

You can use this circle set up for both Full Moons in Aquarius. On each of these Full Moons, we are working with the elements of Air from Aquarius and Fire from Leo. Feel into these elements when creating your space. When Fire meets Air, sparks fly. Choose a space that feels grounded and connected to Mother Earth to help contain the Fire element, but also allow the Air element to breathe new life into your ritual space. You can practice alone or in community; it's entirely up to you. Due to the nature of these Full Moons, you may want to spend the first one with others, while honoring the second one alone. Aquarius is a very social sign and the energy supports gathering with others. If you practice with other people, be sure to choose people you feel at home with—people who give you a true sense of belonging in their presence.

CIRCLE SET UP

Along with the Earth element, incorporate the rest of the elements into your space. If possible, build a fire outside, which you can use for a releasing ritual. You can also light candles to represent Fire. For Air, incorporate auric sprays, feathers to fan the smudge sticks, and even wind chimes to hear the air moving around you. Use crystals to help bring in more of the Earth element, and call in energies that align with their vibration. When placing crystals, allow the crystal to choose its location, using your intuition as a guide. Place crystals in the middle of the circle in the form of a crystal grid and around the perimeter of the space.

Crystals that align with the energy of Aquarius are Peacock Ore, Aquamarine, Goldstone, and Kambabla Jasper. They will help you feel into your unique talent and contribution to the collective. Crystals for Leo are Morganite, Tiger's Eye, Citrine, and Carnelian. They will help you love yourself unconditionally and express your true creativity. You can also incorporate flowers for both Aquarius and Leo, including gladiolas, bird of paradise, and carnations. Bring in the element of Water through a room diffuser, a vase, or a metal bowl containing water. Gather all of your supplies and start to build your circle.

Create an outline with your objects, anchoring the four directions—North, South, East, and West—with either a crystal or candle. If you are creating an altar, set it up in the westerly part of the circle, as this direction helps energies release. On your altar you can place pictures of images that inspire or guide you. Also place items that represent your past or things you want to leave behind. Additionally, place candles and crystals here that facilitate release, such as Obsidian or Shungite. Once the perimeter is set, cleanse the area with a dried herb. For the eclectic energy of Aquarius, try using sweetgrass or rosemary, or both. Begin cleansing at the easterly point, moving to the South, West, and North, then back to the East. Imagine a white light encasing the circle, protecting it from any external energies. Before your guests enter, cleanse them too from head to toe. Don't forget to cleanse yourself. Once you have all entered the circle, pause for a moment to let the energy settle before you begin.

Follow your intuitive guidance when leading a circle. Begin by having each member introduce themself. Talk about the astrological energy of the day and how it is affecting each one of you. Share and learn from each other about your unique experiences with this Full Moon. Give plenty of space for each person to speak. Follow your conversation with the meditation practice in this book to calm the mind. You can then explore the rest of the practices. Do them alone, and share as much or as little as you wish with the group. Go over the questions and continue to learn from each other's perspectives. Finally, pull some cards to tune into your intuitive guidance.

After you've completed the practices, take three pieces of paper. On one, write something you are releasing from your past this Full Moon. On the second, write an intention you are calling in that will help you move forward on your path. On the third, write what you are grateful for tonight. Gather all the releasing notes and either burn them (safely) or rip them to shreds. Gather the intention notes and place them under a crystal in the most easterly corner of your home. Leave them there for a week. Pass the gratitude notes to the person on the left, then have everyone take their neighbor's home. Sharing in others' gratitude is a beautiful way to merge our energy into the collective. End the circle by giving thanks to everyone who attended and to yourself for showing up.

THE WORLD IS A REFLECTION OF THE FREQUENCY YOU EMIT. USE YOUR POWER WISELY.

SPIRIT DAUGHTER

AQUARIUS PRACTICES

This Full Moon is an opportunity to understand our energetic field and the frequency we emit. We are energetic beings. From our cells to the electrical signals they produce, we are a walking energetic system. Part of that system is an energetic field that extends far past the physical body. This field connects with other energetic fields, interacting without our conscious knowledge. The center of our energetic field is the heart. It radiates a frequency greater than any other part of our bodies.

Your energetic field carries frequencies just like a radio or light source. You vibrate at a certain frequency, and that affects the energy you transmit through your energetic field. You have higher and lower frequencies. These frequencies are a product of your thoughts, emotions, and subconscious patterns. For instance, when you focus on gratitude you raise your vibration and send out a higher frequency. Likewise, when you focus on negative thinking, you lower your vibration and send out a lower frequency. Frequencies are not necessarily good or bad; they are just a product of your vibrational state. Throughout the day, your frequency will shift and change depending on how you feel, what you are doing, and who you are with.

Your frequency also plays into your ability to manifest your visions. Like attracts like in the world of energy. When you put out a frequency based in abundance, you attract more abundance. When you exist in a frequency of love, you attract love back to yourself. You also attract more things to help you stay in that frequency. For instance, when you exist in a frequency of gratitude, you attract more to be grateful for. You attract what you emit. giving you more control over your life.

Once you become aware that you are an energetic being, you can begin to refine your frequency and change your life. It all starts with your vibration, and that is a product of your focus. It's important to set your vibrational state each day, just like you pick out an outfit or plan your meals. You can learn to be intentional in your vibration instead of letting it be a byproduct of random thoughts and emotions. You will always have thoughts and emotions that seem out of your control. Once you understand your power to set your vibration, no thought or emotion can sway it.

The simplest way to set your vibration and frequency each day is to write a gratitude list. Through writing this list, you train your mind to focus on what you have in your life, shifting your vibration. You can also create a list on what you love in your life, or the abundance available to you. You can choose what to focus your energy on each day, but know that it's a choice. What you choose to tune into informs your energetic field and its outward-flowing frequency. As you go about your day, things will arise, but your energy will know where to return once you set it.

When we emit a higher frequency, we raise the vibration of the world through the interconnected web of our energetic fields. Our energy has the power to raise other people's frequency. As more people learn to intentionally set their frequency, the vibration of the planet elevates. Ultimately, love is the highest vibration. The closer society can get to existing in the frequency, the closer we will get to the Age of Aquarius—a time of love, oneness, and equality for all.

We also get closer to living in a world where abundance and gratitude are more prevalent than scarcity and selfishness. As the vibration of the world elevates, solutions to our current global issues surface with more ease. Each person strengthens their capacity to call in energy to help solve problems with their elevated frequency. We can break through old paradigms and integrate new ones based in love and respect for the Earth and all of her inhabitants. These may seem like lofty concepts, but the world is ready for them. The Age of Aquarius and the influence of Uranus are asking us to invent a new way of being—a way of being that revolves around energy.

AQUARIUS PRACTICES

The following practices are designed to help you understand and work with your energetic field. They help you release the lower frequencies that you may be holding and focus on the higher ones you are capable of achieving in your field. If you feel lost at any time, return to love.

1. We all have things that lower our frequency. What common emotions drain you and lower your vibrational state?

_____

_____

_____

_____

_____

_____

_____

_____

_____

2. What people in your life lower your vibrational state by disempowering you, pulling you into gossip, controlling you, or making you feel bad about yourself?

_____

_____

_____

_____

_____

_____

_____

_____

_____

_____

_____

AQUARIUS PRACTICES

3. What behaviors lower your vibrational state? These may be acts you do alone or with others. It could also include addictions of any kind, comparing yourself to others, or not loving yourself enough.

_____

_____

_____

_____

_____

_____

_____

_____

_____

_____

_____

_____

4. What does it feel like when your vibration is lowered? What things happen, or don't happen, in your life?

_____

_____

_____

_____

_____

_____

_____

_____

_____

_____

AQUARIUS PRACTICES

5. What emotions lift you up and raise your vibrational state? Where do they come from? How can you bring more of them into your life?

6. What people raise your vibration? How do they raise it? Is this something you can do for yourself?

AQUARIUS PRACTICES

7. What behaviors raise your vibration? These may include healthy habits like getting enough sleep or remembering to take breaks and enjoy the sunset when you've overworked yourself.

_____

_____

_____

_____

_____

_____

_____

_____

_____

_____

_____

_____

8. What does it feel like when your vibrational state is elevated? What happens in your life? Do you feel more in the flow?

_____

_____

_____

_____

_____

_____

_____

_____

_____

_____

_____

AQUARIUS PRACTICES

9. What shifts your vibration from low to high? If you don't know, are you willing to experiment with practices like making a gratitude list?

AQUARIUS PRACTICES

10. Imagine that you could live in a higher frequency of love, gratitude, and abundance each day. What would this feel like? What would your life look like? How could you lift the vibration of everyone around you?

_____

_____

_____

_____

_____

_____

_____

_____

_____

_____

_____

_____

_____

_____

_____

_____

_____

_____

_____

_____

_____

_____

_____

_____

_____

_____

32

LAST QUARTER
IN GEMINI

AUGUST 30TH

Last Quarter Moon occurs when the Moon makes it to the last quarter of the lunar cycle, completing her journey around the Earth back to the Sun. On the Last Quarter Moon, we see a Half Moon in our sky, signifying a 90° separation, or square aspect, between the Sun and the Moon. Squares bring up friction and often crises in the energetic body. They feel tense to us, and we can either choose to resist them or work with the energy presented. If we do choose to lean into the energy and opportunity of the Last Quarter Moon, we tap into a powerful force of release. The Last Quarter Moon's energy encourages us to surrender to what we cannot control and let go as we make space for new energy. There is often an epiphany at this stage of the lunar cycle, where we realize the person we can become if we can finally release an old pattern, emotion, or attachment.

The journey of the Last Quarter Moon is not always an easy one; we must be willing to confront places of resistance within ourselves. These are the areas that hold onto energies that are no longer serving our highest visions. We may feel a loss during this time or even some grief for the things we are releasing. Embrace these feelings, knowing they are part of the process of transformation. Also know that in order to call in new energies, you must let go of the things that block you or lower your frequency, even if they feel comfortable. Trust the process of your release and embrace the witness consciousness to help you through this time.

Gemini flavors this Last Quarter Moon with the Moon being positioned in her stars and the Sun now in Virgo. Gemini and Virgo are both ruled by the planet Mercury, which tends to quicken our minds and our energy. Take time to feel grounded this day if your mind races or anxious energy tries to take over. Utilize breathing techniques to center yourself and steady your vibration as we move through this Moon.

Gemini gives us the gift of survey. Her energy compels us to look at every aspect of our lives and take stock. Gemini is an Air energy and allows us to see the different pieces of our lives and the bigger picture. She fuels our curiosity and helps open our minds to new possibilities and perspectives. Align with Gemini this Last Quarter Moon to question how different energies, situations, people, and projects are fitting together in the intricate web that is you. For the pieces that don't seem to be aligning, decide to either adjust them or release them with ease. Feel into your intuition this Last Quarter Moon. The Sun still in Virgo can help you decide where to continue to work and where to create space for new energies to enter. Try not to overthink this process. Feel the element of Air helping you flow freely through the pieces of your life while you remain open to what new adventures may be around the corner.

On this Last Quarter Moon, try cleansing with a smudge stick, like Palo Santo. Smudging is a great way to cleanse with Air and align further with Gemini's qualities. It also incorporates the Earth element, which will pair well with the Sun in Virgo. Stand outside or in a well-ventilated room with an abundance of air flow. Light the smudge stick and let it burn until it starts to smoke. Have a dish available to catch the ashes. As the stick begins to smoke, think about the energies you are ready to release. Form three releasing statements that declare what you are sending back to the Earth. Repeat these statements as you cleanse yourself with the smudge stick. Starting at your head, circle around your body, including your arms, with the smoke. Be sure to smudge even the bottoms of your feet. Once you are finished, draw the smoke up from the ground to above your head three times. Imagine you are guiding all of the released energy upward and away from you so it can be carried off into the wind. Put the stick out in the dish and take three deep breaths as you welcome new Air, and energy, into your body.

AFFIRMATIONS

Write down energies the energies you want to emit to the world. Also write the energies you wish to call back in and attract through the freqeuncy you emit.

_____

_____

_____

_____

_____

_____

_____

_____

_____

_____

_____

Now write three to five affirmations using the energies listed above. Create "I am statements," which you can tell yourself to shift the vibration you emit and attract.

_____

_____

_____

_____

_____

_____

_____

_____

_____

_____

_____

_____

HAPPY
FULL MOON!

Thank you to everyone who supported and purchased this workbook.

Special Thanks to Rebecca Reitz (rebeccareitz.com, @becca_reitz) for her beautiful artwork on the cover, page 2, 4, 6, 8, 10, 14, 16, 18, 32.

For a monthly subscription contact hello@spiritdaughter.com or visit www.spiritdaughter.com.

Disclaimer: The exercises and yoga sequences in this book are physical activities that should be performed carefully to avoid injury. You agree to accept all risks and release Spirit Daughter and any guest instructors from any and all liabilities. Please take care and enjoy.

Follow along our journey on IG:
@spiritdaughter

We always love seeing your photos & hearing about your experiences with the workbooks! Tag us to be featured on our community page:
@spiritdaughtercollective